ABOUT MAGIC READERS

ABDO continues its commitment to quality books with the nonfiction Magic Readers series. This series includes three levels of books to help students progress to being independent readers while learning factual information. Different levels are intended to reflect the stages of reading in the early grades, helping to select the best level for each individual student.

level 1

Level 1: Books with short sentences and familiar words or patterns to share with children who are beginning to understand how letters and sounds go together.

level 2

Level 2: Books with longer words and sentences and more complex language patterns with less repetition for progressing readers who are practicing common words and letter sounds.

level 3

Level 3: Books with more developed language and vocabulary for transitional readers who are using strategies to figure out unknown words and are ready to learn information more independently.

These nonfiction readers are aligned with the Common Core State Standards progression of literacy, following the sequence of skills and increasing the difficulty of language while engaging the curious minds of young children. These books also reflect the increasing importance of reading informational material in the early grades. They encourage children to read for fun and to learn!

Hannah E. Tolles, MA Reading Specialist

www.abdopublishing.com

Published by Magic Wagon, a division of ABDO, PO Box 398166, Minneapolis, Minnesota 55439. Copyright © 2015 by Abdo Consulting Group, Inc. International copyrights reserved in all countries. No part of this book may be reproduced in any form without written permission from the publisher. Magic Readers™ is a trademark and logo of Magic Wagon.

Printed in the United States of America, North Mankato, Minnesota.
062014
092014

Cover Photo: Thinkstock
Interior Photos: Getty Images, iStockphoto, National Geographic, Science Source, Shutterstock, Thinkstock, Wikipedia Common

Written and edited by Rochelle Baltzer, Heidi M. D. Elston, Megan M. Gunderson, and Bridget O'Brien
Illustrated by Candice Keimig
Designed by Candice Keimig and Jillian O'Brien

Library of Congress Cataloging-in-Publication Data

Elston, Heidi M. D., 1979- author.
  Snakes eat and grow / Heidi M.D. Elston [and three others] ; designed and illustrated by Candice Keimig.
    pages cm. -- (Magic readers. Level 2)
  Audience: Ages 5-8.
  ISBN 978-1-62402-070-4
1. Rattlesnakes--Juvenile literature. 2. Snakes--Infancy--Juvenile literature. I. Keimig, Candice, illustrator. II. Title.
  QL666.O69E474 2015
  597.96'38--dc23
                      2014013776

Magic Readers

level
2

Snakes
Eat and Grow

By Heidi M. D. Elston
Illustrated photos by Candice Keimig

Magic Readers

An Imprint of Magic Wagon
www.abdopublishing.com

This is a baby snake.

It is a baby rattlesnake.

A mother snake has 10 to 20
babies.

Each baby can be 1 foot long!

Baby snakes live on their own.

Their mom and dad don't need to care for them.

First, a baby snake sticks out its tongue.

It tastes the air!

A newborn rattlesnake does not go far.

It stays until it sheds its skin.

A rattlesnake sheds its skin as it grows.

Each time, its rattle gets longer.

Snakes need to eat.

They are good hunters.

A rattlesnake has fangs.

It uses them to kill its food.

Rattlesnakes eat lizards and birds.

They also eat mice and toads
and bugs.

Big rattlesnakes can be 8 feet long!

They can grow to 10 pounds.

Rattlesnakes can live for 25 years.